Poetry Library
KV-014-027
119620

SONNETS

BY

EDWIN ARLINGTON ROBINSON

COLLECTED POEMS

Avon's Harvest
Captain Craig
The Children of the Night
Lancelot
The Man Against the Sky
Merlin
The Town Down the River
The Three Taverns

DIONYSUS IN DOUBT

THE MAN WHO DIED TWICE

THE PORCUPINE

ROMAN BARTHOLOW

THE THREE TAVERNS

VAN ZORN

TRISTRAM

SONNETS

1889-1927

EDWIN ARLINGTON ROBINSON

THE MACMILLAN COMPANY
NEW YORK
1928

Set up and electrotyped
Published October 1928 *by The Macmillan Company*

Printed in
THE UNITED STATES OF AMERICA
C

THE AUTHOR'S THANKS ARE DUE TO MESSRS. CHARLES SCRIBNER'S SONS FOR THEIR FRIENDLY COOPERATION IN THE ARRANGEMENT OF THIS FIRST COLLECTION OF THESE SONNETS.

CONTENTS

CONTENTS—*Continued*

CONTENTS—*Continued*

CONTENTS—*Continued*

SONNETS

CALVARY

FRIENDLESS and faint, with martyred steps and slow,
Faint for the flesh, but for the spirit free,
Stung by the mob that came to see the show,
The Master toiled along to Calvary;
We gibed him, as he went, with houndish glee,
Till his dimmed eyes for us did overflow;
We cursed his vengeless hands thrice wretchedly,—
And this was nineteen hundred years ago.

But after nineteen hundred years the shame
Still clings, and we have not made good the loss
That outraged faith has entered in his name.
Ah, when shall come love's courage to be strong!
Tell me, O Lord—tell me, O Lord, how long
Are we to keep Christ writhing on the cross!

DEAR FRIENDS

DEAR friends, reproach me not for what I do,
Nor counsel me, nor pity me; nor say
That I am wearing half my life away
For bubble-work that only fools pursue.
And if my bubbles be too small for you,
Blow bigger then your own: the games we play
To fill the frittered minutes of a day,
Good glasses are to read the spirit through.

And whoso reads may get him some shrewd skill;
And some unprofitable scorn resign,
To praise the very thing that he deplores.
So, friends (dear friends), remember, if you will,
The shame I win for singing is all mine,
The gold I miss for dreaming is all yours.

THE STORY OF THE ASHES AND THE FLAME

No MATTER why, nor whence, nor when she came,
There was her place. No matter what men said,
No matter what she was; living or dead,
Faithful or not, he loved her all the same.
The story was as old as human shame,
But ever since that lonely night she fled,
With books to blind him, he had only read
The story of the ashes and the flame.

There she was always coming pretty soon
To fool him back, with penitent scared eyes
That had in them the laughter of the moon
For baffled lovers, and to make him think—
Before she gave him time enough to wink—
Her kisses were the keys to Paradise.

AMARYLLIS

ONCE, when I wandered in the woods alone,
An old man tottered up to me and said,
"Come, friend, and see the grave that I have made
For Amaryllis." There was in the tone
Of his complaint such quaver and such moan
That I took pity on him and obeyed,
And long stood looking where his hands had laid
An ancient woman, shrunk to skin and bone.

Far out beyond the forest I could hear
The calling of loud progress, and the bold
Incessant scream of commerce ringing clear;
But though the trumpets of the world were glad,
It made me lonely and it made me sad
To think that Amaryllis had grown old.

ZOLA

BECAUSE he puts the compromising chart
Of hell before your eyes, you are afraid;
Because he counts the price that you have paid
For innocence, and counts it from the start,
You loathe him. But he sees the human heart
Of God meanwhile, and in His hand has weighed
Your squeamish and emasculate crusade
Against the grim dominion of his art.

Never until we conquer the uncouth
Connivings of our shamed indifference
(We call it Christian faith) are we to scan
The racked and shrieking hideousness of Truth
To find, in hate's polluted self-defence,
Throbbing, the pulse, the divine heart of man.

THE PITY OF THE LEAVES

VENGEFUL across the cold November moors,
Loud with ancestral shame there came the bleak
Sad wind that shrieked, and answered with a shriek,
Reverberant through lonely corridors.
The old man heard it; and he heard, perforce,
Words out of lips that were no more to speak—
Words of the past that shook the old man's cheek
Like dead, remembered footsteps on old floors.

And then there were the leaves that plagued him so!
The brown, thin leaves that on the stones outside
Skipped with a freezing whisper. Now and then
They stopped, and stayed there—just to let him know
How dead they were; but if the old man cried,
They fluttered off like withered souls of men.

AARON STARK

WITHAL a meagre man was Aaron Stark,
Cursed and unkempt, shrewd, shrivelled, and
morose.
A miser was he, with a miser's nose,
And eyes like little dollars in the dark.
His thin, pinched mouth was nothing but a mark;
And when he spoke there came like sullen blows
Through scattered fangs a few snarled words and
close,
As if a cur were chary of its bark.

Glad for the murmur of his hard renown,
Year after year he shambled through the town,
A loveless exile moving with a staff;
And oftentimes there crept into his ears
A sound of alien pity, touched with tears,—
And then (and only then) did Aaron laugh.

THE GARDEN

THERE is a fenceless garden overgrown
With buds and blossoms and all sorts of leaves;
And once, among the roses and the sheaves,
The Gardener and I were there alone.
He led me to the plot where I had thrown
The fennel of my days on wasted ground,
And in that riot of sad weeds I found
The fruitage of a life that was my own.

My life! Ah, yes, there was my life, indeed!
And there were all the lives of humankind;
And they were like a book that I could read,
Whose every leaf, miraculously signed,
Outrolled itself from Thought's eternal seed,
Love-rooted in God's garden of the mind.

CLIFF KLINGENHAGEN

CLIFF KLINGENHAGEN had me in to dine
With him one day; and after soup and meat,
And all the other things there were to eat,
Cliff took two glasses and filled one with wine
And one with wormwood. Then, without a sign
For me to choose at all, he took the draught
Of bitterness himself, and lightly quaffed
It off, and said the other one was mine.

And when I asked him what the deuce he meant
By doing that, he only looked at me
And smiled, and said it was a way of his.
And though I know the fellow, I have spent
Long time a-wondering when I shall be
As happy as Cliff Klingenhagen is.

CHARLES CARVILLE'S EYES

A MELANCHOLY face Charles Carville had,
But not so melancholy as it seemed,
When once you knew him, for his mouth redeemed
His insufficient eyes, forever sad:
In them there was no life-glimpse, good or bad,
Nor joy nor passion in them ever gleamed;
His mouth was all of him that ever beamed,
His eyes were sorry, but his mouth was glad.

He never was a fellow that said much,
And half of what he did say was not heard
By many of us: we were out of touch
With all his whims and all his theories
Till he was dead, so those blank eyes of his
Might speak them. Then we heard them, every word.

THE DEAD VILLAGE

HERE there is death. But even here, they say,
Here where the dull sun shines this afternoon
As desolate as ever the dead moon
Did glimmer on dead Sardis, men were gay;
And there were little children here to play,
With small soft hands that once did keep in tune
The strings that stretch from heaven, till too soon
The change came, and the music passed away.

Now there is nothing but the ghosts of things,—
No life, no love, no children, and no men;
And over the forgotten place there clings
The strange and unrememberable light
That is in dreams. The music failed, and then
God frowned, and shut the village from His sight.

TWO SONNETS

I

JUST as I wonder at the twofold screen
Of twisted innocence that you would plait
For eyes that uncourageously await
The coming of a kingdom that has been,
So do I wonder what God's love can mean
To you that all so strangely estimate
The purpose and the consequent estate
Of one short shuddering step to the Unseen.

No, I have not your backward faith to shrink
Lone-faring from the doorway of God's home
To find Him in the names of buried men;
Nor your ingenious recreance to think
We cherish, in the life that is to come,
The scattered features of dead friends again.

TWO SONNETS

II

NEVER until our souls are strong enough
To plunge into the crater of the Scheme—
Triumphant in the flash there to redeem
Love's hansel and forevermore to slough,
Like cerements at a played-out masque, the rough
And reptile skins of us whereon we set
The stigma of scared years—are we to get
Where atoms and the ages are one stuff.

Nor ever shall we know the cursed waste
Of life in the beneficence divine
Of starlight and of sunlight and soul-shine
That we have squandered in sin's frail distress,
Till we have drunk, and trembled at the taste,
The mead of Thought's prophetic endlessness.

THE CLERKS

I DID not think that I should find them there
When I came back again; but there they stood,
As in the days they dreamed of when young blood
Was in their cheeks and women called them fair.
Be sure, they met me with an ancient air,—
And yes, there was a shop-worn brotherhood
About them; but the men were just as good,
And just as human as they ever were.

And you that ache so much to be sublime,
And you that feed yourselves with your descent,
What comes of all your visions and your fears?
Poets and kings are but the clerks of Time,
Tiering the same dull webs of discontent,
Clipping the same sad alnage of the years.

FLEMING HELPHENSTINE

At first I thought there was a superfine
Persuasion in his face; but the free glow
That filled it when he stopped and cried, "Hollo!"
Shone joyously, and so I let it shine.
He said his name was Fleming Helphenstine,
But be that as it may;—I only know
He talked of this and that and So-and-So,
And laughed and chaffed like any friend of mine.

But soon, with a queer, quick frown, he looked at me,
And I looked hard at him; and there we gazed
In a strained way that made us cringe and wince:
Then, with a wordless clogged apology
That sounded half confused and half amazed,
He dodged,—and I have never seen him since.

THOMAS HOOD

THE man who cloaked his bitterness within
This winding-sheet of puns and pleasantries,
God never gave to look with common eyes
Upon a world of anguish and of sin:
His brother was the branded man of Lynn;
And there are woven with his jollities
The nameless and eternal tragedies
That render hope and hopelessness akin.

We laugh, and crown him; but anon we feel
A still chord sorrow-swept,—a weird unrest;
And thin dim shadows home to midnight steal,
As if the very ghost of mirth were dead—
As if the joys of time to dreams had fled,
Or sailed away with Ines to the West.

HORACE TO LEUCONOË

I PRAY you not, Leuconoë, to pore
With unpermitted eyes on what may be
Appointed by the gods for you and me,
Nor on Chaldean figures any more.
'T were infinitely better to implore
The present only:—whether Jove decree
More winters yet to come, or whether he
Make even this, whose hard, wave-eaten shore
Shatters the Tuscan seas to-day, the last—
Be wise withal, and rack your wine, nor fill
Your bosom with large hopes; for while I sing,
The envious close of time is narrowing;
So seize the day, or ever it be past,
And let the morrow come for what it will.

REUBEN BRIGHT

Because he was a butcher and thereby
Did earn an honest living (and did right),
I would not have you think that Reuben Bright
Was any more a brute than you or I;
For when they told him that his wife must die,
He stared at them, and shook with grief and fright,
And cried like a great baby half that night,
And made the women cry to see him cry.

And after she was dead, and he had paid
The singers and the sexton and the rest,
He packed a lot of things that she had made
Most mournfully away in an old chest
Of hers, and put some chopped-up cedar boughs
In with them, and tore down the slaughter-house.

THE ALTAR

Alone, remote, nor witting where I went,
I found an altar builded in a dream—
A fiery place, whereof there was a gleam
So swift, so searching, and so eloquent
Of upward promise, that love's murmur, blent
With sorrow's warning, gave but a supreme
Unending impulse to that human stream
Whose flood was all for the flame's fury bent.

Alas! I said,—the world is in the wrong.
But the same quenchless fever of unrest
That thrilled the foremost of that martyred throng
Thrilled me, and I awoke . . . and was the same
Bewildered insect plunging for the flame
That burns, and must burn somehow for the best.

THE TAVERN

WHENEVER I go by there nowadays
And look at the rank weeds and the strange grass,
The torn blue curtains and the broken glass,
I seem to be afraid of the old place;
And something stiffens up and down my face,
For all the world as if I saw the ghost
Of old Ham Amory, the murdered host,
With his dead eyes turned on me all aglaze.

The Tavern has a story, but no man
Can tell us what it is. We only know
That once long after midnight, years ago,
A stranger galloped up from Tilbury Town,
Who brushed, and scared, and all but overran
That skirt-crazed reprobate, John Evereldown.

SONNET

OH, FOR a poet—for a beacon bright
To rift this changeless glimmer of dead gray;
To spirit back the Muses, long astray,
And flush Parnassus with a newer light;
To put these little sonnet-men to flight
Who fashion, in a shrewd mechanic way,
Songs without souls, that flicker for a day,
To vanish in irrevocable night.

What does it mean, this barren age of ours?
Here are the men, the women, and the flowers,
The seasons, and the sunset, as before.
What does it mean? Shall there not one arise
To wrench one banner from the western skies,
And mark it with his name for evermore?

GEORGE CRABBE

GIVE him the darkest inch your shelf allows,
Hide him in lonely garrets, if you will,
But his hard, human pulse is throbbing still
With the sure strength that fearless truth endows.
In spite of all fine science disavows,
Of his plain excellence and stubborn skill
There yet remains what fashion cannot kill,
Though years have thinned the laurel from his brows.

Whether or not we read him, we can feel
From time to time the vigor of his name
Against us like a finger for the shame
And emptiness of what our souls reveal
In books that are as altars where we kneel
To consecrate the flicker, not the flame.

CREDO

I CANNOT find my way: there is no star
In all the shrouded heavens anywhere;
And there is not a whisper in the air
Of any living voice but one so far
That I can hear it only as a bar
Of lost, imperial music, played when fair
And angel fingers wove, and unaware,
Dead leaves to garlands where no roses are.

No, there is not a glimmer, nor a call,
For one that welcomes, welcomes when he fears,
The black and awful chaos of the night;
For through it all—above, beyond it all—
I know the far-sent message of the years,
I feel the coming glory of the Light.

ON THE NIGHT OF A FRIEND'S WEDDING

IF EVER I am old and all alone,
I shall have killed one grief, at any rate;
For then, thank God, I shall not have to wait
Much longer for the sheaves that I have sown.
The devil only knows what I have done,
But here I am, and here are six or eight
Good friends, who most ingenuously prate
About my songs to such and such a one.

But everything is all askew to-night,—
As if the time were come, or almost come,
For their untenanted mirage of me
To lose itself and crumble out of sight,
Like a tall ship that floats above the foam
A little while, and then breaks utterly.

SONNET

The master and the slave go hand in hand,
Though touch be lost. The poet is a slave,
And there be kings do sorrowfully crave
The joyance that a scullion may command.
But, ah, the sonnet-slave must understand
The mission of his bondage, or the grave
May clasp his bones, or ever he shall save
The perfect word that is the poet's wand.

The sonnet is a crown, whereof the rhymes
Are for Thought's purest gold the jewel-stones;
But shapes and echoes that are never done
Will haunt the workship, as regret sometimes
Will bring with human yearning to sad thrones
The crash of battles that are never won.

VERLAINE

WHY do you dig like long-clawed scavengers
To touch the covered corpse of him that fled
The uplands for the fens, and rioted
Like a sick satyr with doom's worshippers?
Come! let the grass grow there; and leave his verse
To tell the story of the life he led.
Let the man go: let the dead flesh be dead,
And let the worms be its biographers.

Song sloughs away the sin to find redress
In art's complete remembrance: nothing clings
For long but laurel to the stricken brow
That felt the Muse's finger: nothing less
Than hell's fulfillment of the end of things
Can blot the star that shines on Paris now.

SONNET

WHEN we can all so excellently give
The measure of love's wisdom with a blow,
Why can we not in turn receive it so,
And end this murmur for the life we live?
And when we do so frantically strive
To win strange faith, why do we shun to know
That in love's elemental over-glow
God's wholeness gleams with light superlative?

Oh, brother men, if you have eyes at all,
Look at a branch, a bird, a child, a rose,
Or anything God ever made that grows,—
Nor let the smallest vision of it slip,
Till you may read, as on Belshazzar's wall,
The glory of eternal partnership.

SUPREMACY

THERE is a drear and lonely tract of hell
From all the common gloom removed afar:
A flat, sad land it is, where shadows are,
Whose lorn estate my verse may never tell.
I walked among them and I knew them well:
Men I had slandered on life's little star
For churls and sluggards; and I knew the scar
Upon their brows of woe ineffable.

But as I went majestic on my way,
Into the dark they vanished, one by one,
Till, with a shaft of God's eternal day,
The dream of all my glory was undone,—
And, with a fool's importunate dismay,
I heard the dead men singing in the sun.

THE TORRENT

I FOUND a torrent falling in a glen
Where the sun's light shone silvered and leaf-split;
The boom, the foam, and the mad flash of it
All made a magic symphony; but when
I thought upon the coming of hard men
To cut those patriarchal trees away,
And turn to gold the silver of that spray,
I shuddered. Yet a gladness now and then
Did wake me to myself till I was glad
In earnest, and was welcoming the time
For screaming saws to sound above the chime
Of idle waters, and for me to know
The jealous visionings that I had had
Were steps to the great place where trees and torrents go.

L'ENVOI

Now in a thought, now in a shadowed word,
Now in a voice that thrills eternity,
Ever there comes an onward phrase to me
Of some transcendent music I have heard;
No piteous thing by soft hands dulcimered,
No trumpet crash of blood-sick victory,
But a glad strain of some vast harmony
That no brief mortal touch has ever stirred.

There is no music in the world like this,
No character wherewith to set it down,
No kind of instrument to make it sing.
No kind of instrument? Ah, yes, there is;
And after time and place are overthrown,
God's touch will keep its one chord quivering.

THE SAGE

FOREGUARDED and unfevered and serene,
Back to the perilous gates of Truth he went—
Back to fierce wisdom and the Orient,
To the Dawn that is, that shall be, and has been:
Previsioned of the madness and the mean,
He stood where Asia, crowned with ravishment,
The curtain of Love's inner shrine had rent,
And after had gone scarred by the Unseen.

There at his touch there was a treasure chest,
And in it was a gleam, but not of gold;
And on it, like a flame, these words were scrolled:
"I keep the mintage of Eternity.
Who comes to take one coin may take the rest,
And all may come—but not without the key."

ERASMUS

WHEN he protested, not too solemnly,
That for a world's achieving maintenance
The crust of overdone divinity
Lacked aliment, they called it recreance;
And when he chose through his own glass to scan
Sick Europe, and reduced, unyieldingly,
The monk within the cassock to the man
Within the monk, they called it heresy.

And when he made so perilously bold
As to be scattered forth in black and white,
Good fathers looked askance at him and rolled
Their inward eyes in anguish and affright;
There were some of them did shake at what was told,
And they shook best who knew that he was right.

THE GROWTH OF "LORRAINE"

I

WHILE I stood listening, discreetly dumb,
Lorraine was having the last word with me:
"I know," she said, "I know it, but you see
Some creatures are born fortunate, and some
Are born to be found out and overcome,—
Born to be slaves, to let the rest go free;
And if I'm one of them (and I must be)
You may as well forget me and go home.

"You tell me not to say these things, I know,
But I should never try to be content:
I've gone too far; the life would be too slow.
Some could have done it—some girls have the
stuff;
But I can't do it: I don't know enough.
I'm going to the devil."—And she went.

THE GROWTH OF "LORRAINE"

II

I did not half believe her when she said
That I should never hear from her again;
Nor when I found a letter from Lorraine,
Was I surprised or grieved at what I read:
"Dear friend, when you find this, I shall be dead.
You are too far away to make me stop.
They say that one drop—think of it, one drop!—
Will be enough,—but I'll take five instead.

"You do not frown because I call you friend,
For I would have you glad that I still keep
Your memory, and even at the end—
Impenitent, sick, shattered—cannot curse
The love that flings, for better or for worse,
This worn-out, cast-out flesh of mine to sleep."

THE WOMAN AND THE WIFE

I The Explanation

"You thought we knew," she said, "but we were
wrong.
This we can say, the rest we do not say;
Nor do I let you throw yourself away
Because you love me. Let us both be strong,
And we shall find in sorrow, before long,
Only the price Love ruled that we should pay:
The dark is at the end of every day,
And silence is the end of every song.

"You ask me for one proof that I speak right,
But I can answer only what I know;
You look for just one lie to make black white,
But I can tell you only what is true—
God never made me for the wife of you.
This we can say,—believe me! . . . Tell me so!"

THE WOMAN AND THE WIFE

II The Anniversary

"Give me the truth, whatever it may be.
You thought we knew, now tell me what you miss:
You are the one to tell me what it is—
You are a man, and you have married me.
What is it worth to-night that you can see
More marriage in the dream of one dead kiss
Than in a thousand years of life like this?
Passion has turned the lock, Pride keeps the key.

"Whatever I have said or left unsaid,
Whatever I have done or left undone,—
Tell me. Tell me the truth . . . Are you afraid?
Do you think that Love was ever fed with lies
But hunger lived thereafter in his eyes?
Do you ask me to take moonlight for the sun?"

DORICHA

(*Posidippus*)

So now the very bones of you are gone
Where they were dust and ashes long ago;
And there was the last ribbon you tied on
To bind your hair, and that is dust also;
And somewhere there is dust that was of old
A soft and scented garment that you wore—
The same that once till dawn did closely fold
You in with fair Charaxus, fair no more.

But Sappho, and the white leaves of her song,
Will make your name a word for all to learn,
And all to love thereafter, even while
It's but a name; and this will be as long
As there are distant ships that will return
Again to Naucratis and to the Nile.

LEFFINGWELL

I The Lure

No, no,—forget your Cricket and your Ant,
For I shall never set my name to theirs
That now bespeak the very sons and heirs
Incarnate of Queen Gossip and King Cant.
The case of Leffingwell is mixed, I grant,
And futile seems the burden that he bears;
But are we sounding his forlorn affairs
Who brand him parasite and sycophant?

I tell you, Leffingwell was more than these;
And if he proved a rather sorry knight,
What quiverings in the distance of what light
May not have lured him with high promises,
And then gone down?—He may have been
deceived;
He may have lied,—he did; and he believed.

LEFFINGWELL

II THE QUICKSTEP

THE dirge is over, the good work is done,
All as he would have had it, and we go;
And we who leave him say we do not know
How much is ended or how much begun.
So men have said before of many a one;
So men may say of us when Time shall throw
Such earth as may be needful to bestow
On you and me the covering hush we shun.

Well hated, better loved, he played and lost,
And left us; and we smile at his arrears;
And who are we to know what it all cost,
Or what we may have wrung from him, the buyer?
The pageant of his failure-laden years
Told ruin of high price. The place was higher.

III Requiescat

We never knew the sorrow or the pain
Within him, for he seemed as one asleep—
Until he faced us with a dying leap,
And with a blast of paramount, profane,
And vehement valediction did explain
To each of us, in words that we shall keep,
Why we were not to wonder or to weep,
Or ever dare to wish him back again.

He may be now an amiable shade,
With merry fellow-phantoms unafraid
Around him—but we do not ask. We know
That he would rise and haunt us horribly,
And be with us o' nights of a certainty.
Did we not hear him when he told us so?

LINGARD AND THE STARS

THE table hurled itself, to our surprise,
At Lingard, and anon rapped eagerly:
"When earth is cold and there is no more sea,
There will be what was Lingard. Otherwise,
Why lure the race to ruin through the skies?
And why have Leffingwell, or Calverly?"—
"I wish the ghost would give his name," said he;
And searching gratitude was in his eyes.

He stood then by the window for a time,
And only after the last midnight chime
Smote the day dead did he say anything:
"Come out, my little one, the stars are bright;
Come out, you lælaps, and inhale the night."
And so he went away with Clavering.

HOW ANNANDALE WENT OUT

"They called it Annandale—and I was there
To flourish, to find words, and to attend:
Liar, physician, hypocrite, and friend,
I watched him; and the sight was not so fair
As one or two that I have seen elsewhere:
An apparatus not for me to mend—
A wreck, with hell between him and the end,
Remained of Annandale; and I was there.

"I knew the ruin as I knew the man;
So put the two together, if you can,
Remembering the worst you know of me.
Now view yourself as I was, on the spot—
With a slight kind of engine. Do you see?
Like this . . . You wouldn't hang me? I thought
not."

ALMA MATER

He knocked, and I beheld him at the door—
A vision for the gods to verify.
"What battered ancientry is this," thought I,
"And when, if ever, did we meet before?"
But ask him as I might, I got no more
For answer than a moaning and a cry:
Too late to parley, but in time to die,
He staggered, and lay shapeless on the floor.

When had I known him? And what brought him
here?
Love, warning, malediction, hunger, fear?
Surely I never thwarted such as he?—
Again, what soiled obscurity was this:
Out of what scum, and up from what abyss,
Had they arrived—these rags of memory?

SHADRACH O'LEARY

O'LEARY was a poet—for a while:
He sang of many ladies frail and fair,
The rolling glory of their golden hair,
And emperors extinguished with a smile.
They foiled his years with many an ancient wile,
And if they limped, O'Leary didn't care:
He turned them loose and had them everywhere,
Undoing saints and senates with their guile.

But this was not the end. A year ago
I met him—and to meet was to admire:
Forgotten were the ladies and the lyre,
And the small, ink-fed Eros of his dream.
By questioning I found a man to know—
A failure spared, a Shadrach of the Gleam.

DOCTOR OF BILLIARDS

OF ALL among the fallen from on high,
We count you last and leave you to regain
Your born dominion of a life made vain
By three spheres of insidious ivory.
You dwindle to the lesser tragedy—
Content, you say. We call, but you remain.
Nothing alive gone wrong could be so plain,
Or quite so blasted with absurdity.

You click away the kingdom that is yours,
And you click off your crown for cap and bells;
You smile, who are still master of the feast,
And for your smile we credit you the least;
But when your false, unhallowed laugh occurs,
We seem to think there may be something else.

THE SUNKEN CROWN

NOTHING will hold him longer—let him go;
Let him go down where others have gone down;
Little he cares whether we smile or frown,
Or if we know, or if we think we know.
The call is on him for his overthrow,
Say we; so let him rise, or let him drown.
Poor fool! He plunges for the sunken crown,
And we—we wait for what the plunge may show.

Well, we are safe enough. Why linger, then?
The watery chance was his, not ours. Poor fool!
Poor truant, poor Narcissus out of school;
Poor jest of Ascalon; poor king of men.
The crown, if he be wearing it, may cool
His arrogance, and he may sleep again.

FOR ARVIA

On Her Fifth Birthday

You Eyes, you large and all-inquiring Eyes,
That look so dubiously into me,
And are not satisfied with what you see,
Tell me the worst and let us have no lies:
Tell me the meaning of your scrutinies,
And of myself. Am I a Mystery?
Am I a Boojum—or just Company?
What do you say? What do you think, You Eyes?

You say not; but you think, beyond a doubt;
And you have the whole world to think about,
With very little time for little things.
So let it be; and let it all be fair—
For you, and for the rest who cannot share
Your gold of unrevealed awakenings.

ANOTHER DARK LADY

THINK not, because I wonder where you fled,
That I would lift a pin to see you there;
You may, for me, be prowling anywhere,
So long as you show not your little head:
No dark and evil story of the dead
Would leave you less pernicious or less fair—
Not even Lilith, with her famous hair;
And Lilith was the devil, I have read.

I cannot hate you, for I loved you then.
The woods were golden then. There was a road
Through beeches; and I said their smooth feet
    showed
Like yours. Truth must have heard me from afar,
For I shall never have to learn again
That yours are cloven as no beech's are.

A SONG AT SHANNON'S

Two men came out of Shannon's, having known
The faces of each other for as long
As they had listened there to an old song,
Sung thinly in a wastrel monotone
By some unhappy night-bird, who had flown
Too many times and with a wing too strong
To save himself, and so done heavy wrong
To more frail elements than his alone.

Slowly away they went, leaving behind
More light than was before them. Neither met
The other's eyes again or said a word.
Each to his loneliness or to his kind,
Went his own way, and with his own regret,
Not knowing what the other may have heard.

SOUVENIR

A VANISHED house that for an hour I knew
By some forgotten chance when I was young
Had once a glimmering window overhung
With honeysuckle wet with evening dew.
Along the path tall dusky dahlias grew,
And shadowy hydrangeas reached and swung
Ferociously; and over me, among
The moths and mysteries, a blurred bat flew.

Somewhere within there were dim presences
Of days that hovered and of years gone by.
I waited, and between their silences
There was an evanescent faded noise;
And though a child, I knew it was the voice
Of one whose occupation was to die.

DISCOVERY

WE TOLD of him as one who should have soared
And seen for us the devastating light
Whereof there is not either day or night,
And shared with us the glamour of the Word
That fell once upon Amos to record
For men at ease in Zion, when the sight
Of ills obscured aggrieved him and the might
Of Hamath was a warning of the Lord.

Assured somehow that he would make us wise,
Our pleasure was to wait; and our surprise
Was hard when we confessed the dry return
Of his regret. For we were still to learn
That earth has not a school where we may go
For wisdom, or for more than we may know.

FIRELIGHT

Ten years together without yet a cloud,
They seek each other's eyes at intervals
Of gratefulness to firelight and four walls
For love's obliteration of the crowd.
Serenely and perennially endowed
And bowered as few may be, their joy recalls
No snake, no sword; and over them there falls
The blessing of what neither says aloud.

Wiser for silence, they were not so glad
Were she to read the graven tale of lines
On the wan face of one somewhere alone;
Nor were they more content could he have had
Her thoughts a moment since of one who shines
Apart, and would be hers if he had known.

THE NEW TENANTS

The day was here when it was his to know
How fared the barriers he had built between
His triumph and his enemies unseen,
For them to undermine and overthrow;
And it was his no longer to forego
The sight of them, insidious and serene,
Where they were delving always and had been
Left always to be vicious and to grow.

And there were the new tenants who had come,
By doors that were left open unawares,
Into his house, and were so much at home
There now that he would hardly have to guess,
By the slow guile of their vindictiveness,
What ultimate insolence would soon be theirs.

INFERENTIAL

ALTHOUGH I saw before me there the face
Of one whom I had honored among men
The least, and on regarding him again
Would not have had him in another place,
He fitted with an unfamiliar grace
The coffin where I could not see him then
As I had seen him and appraised him when
I deemed him unessential to the race.

For there was more of him than what I saw,
And there was on me more than the old awe
That is the common genius of the dead.
I might as well have heard him: "Never mind;
If some of us were not so far behind,
The rest of us were not so far ahead."

THE RAT

As OFTEN as he let himself be seen
We pitied him, or scorned him, or deplored
The inscrutable profusion of the Lord
Who shaped as one of us a thing so mean—
Who made him human when he might have been
A rat, and so been wholly in accord
With any other creature we abhorred
As always useless and not always clean.

Now he is hiding all alone somewhere,
And in a final hole not ready then;
For now he is among those over there
Who are not coming back to us again.
And we who do the fiction of our share,
Say less of rats and rather more of men.

AN EVANGELIST'S WIFE

"Why am I not myself these many days,
You ask? And have you nothing more to ask?
I do you wrong? I do not hear your praise
To God for giving you me to share your task?

"Jealous—of Her? Because her cheeks are pink,
And she has eyes? No, not if she had seven.
If you should only steal an hour to think,
Sometime, there might be less to be forgiven.

"No, you are never cruel. If once or twice
I found you so, I could applaud and sing.
Jealous of—What? You are not very wise.
Does not the good Book tell you anything?

"In David's time poor Michal had to go.
Jealous of God? Well, if you like it so."

DEMOS

I

All you that are enamored of my name
And least intent on what most I require,
Beware; for my design and your desire,
Deplorably, are not as yet the same.
Beware, I say, the failure and the shame
Of losing that for which you now aspire
So blindly, and of hazarding entire
The gift that I was bringing when I came.

Give as I will, I cannot give you sight
Whereby to see that with you there are some
To lead you, and be led. But they are dumb
Before the wrangling and the shrill delight
Of your deliverance that has not come,
And shall not, if I fail you—as I might.

DEMOS

II

So LITTLE have you seen of what awaits
Your fevered glimpse of a democracy
Confused and foiled with an equality
Not equal to the envy it creates,
That you see not how near you are the gates
Of an old king who listens fearfully
To you that are outside and are to be
The noisy lords of imminent estates.

Rather be then your prayer that you shall have
Your kingdom undishonored. Having all,
See not the great among you for the small,
But hear their silence; for the few shall save
The many, or the many are to fall—
Still to be wrangling in a noisy grave.

THE deacon thought. "I know them," he began,
"And they are all you ever heard of them—
Allurable to no sure theorem,
The scorn or the humility of man.
You say 'Can I believe it?'—and I can;
And I'm unwilling even to condemn
The benefaction of a stratagem
Like hers—and I'm a Presbyterian.

"Though blind, with but a wandering hour to live,
He felt the other woman in the fur
That now the wife had on. Could she forgive
All that? Apparently. Her rings were gone,
Of course; and when he found that she had none,
He smiled—as he had never smiled at her."

THE TREE IN PAMELA'S GARDEN

PAMELA was too gentle to deceive
Her roses. "Let the men stay where they are,"
She said, "and if Apollo's avatar
Be one of them, I shall not have to grieve."
And so she made all Tilbury Town believe
She sighed a little more for the North Star
Than over men, and only in so far
As she was in a garden was like Eve.

Her neighbors—doing all that neighbors can
To make romance of reticence meanwhile—
Seeing that she had never loved a man,
Wished Pamela had a cat, or a small bird,
And only would have wondered at her smile
Could they have seen that she had overheard.

VAIN GRATUITIES

NEVER was there a man much uglier
In eyes of other women, or more grim:
"The Lord has filled her chalice to the brim,
So let us pray she's a philosopher,"
They said; and there was more they said of her—
Deeming it, after twenty years with him,
No wonder that she kept her figure slim
And always made you think of lavender.

But she, demure as ever, and as fair,
Almost, as they remembered her before
She found him, would have laughed had she been
there;
And all they said would have been heard no more
Than foam that washes on an island shore
Where there are none to listen or to care.

JOB THE REJECTED

They met, and overwhelming her distrust
With penitence, he praised away her fear;
They married, and Job gave him half a year
To wreck the temple, as we knew he must.
He fumbled hungrily to readjust
A fallen altar, but the road was clear
By which it was her will to disappear
That evening when Job found him in the dust.

Job would have deprecated such a way
Of heaving fuel on a sacred fire,
Yet even the while we saw it going out,
Hardly was Job to find his hour to shout;
And Job was not, so far as we could say,
The confirmation of her soul's desire.

LOST ANCHORS

LIKE a dry fish flung inland far from shore,
There lived a sailor, warped and ocean-browned,
Who told of an old vessel, harbor-drowned
And out of mind a century before,
Where divers, on descending to explore
A legend that had lived its way around
The world of ships, in the dark hulk had found
Anchors, which had been seized and seen no more.

Improving a dry leisure to invest
Their misadventure with a manifest
Analogy that he may read who runs,
The sailor made it old as ocean grass—
Telling of much that once had come to pass
With him, whose mother should have had no sons.

RECALLED

Long after there were none of them alive
About the place—where there is now no place
But a walled hole where fruitless vines embrace
Their parent skeletons that yet survive
In evil thorns—none of us could arrive
At a more cogent answer to their ways
Than one old Isaac in his latter days
Had humor or compassion to contrive.

I mentioned them, and Isaac shook his head:
"The Power that you call yours and I call mine
Extinguished in the last of them a line
That Satan would have disinherited.
When we are done with all but the Divine,
We die." And there was no more to be said.

SMALL knowledge have we that by knowledge met
May not some day be quaint as any told
In almagest or chronicle of old,
Whereat we smile because we are as yet
The last—though not the last who may forget
What cleavings and abrasions manifold
Have marked an armor that was never scrolled
Before for human glory and regret.

With infinite unseen enemies in the way
We have encountered the intangible,
To vanquish where our fathers, who fought well,
Scarce had assumed endurance for a day;
Yet we shall have our darkness, even as they,
And there shall be another tale to tell.

WE PARTED where the old gas-lamp still burned
Under the wayside maple and walked on,
Into the dark, as we had always done;
And I, no doubt, if he had not returned,
Might yet be unaware that he had earned
More than earth gives to many who have won
More than it has to give when they are gone—
As duly and indelibly I learned.

The sum of all that he came back to say
Was little then, and would be less to-day:
With him there were no Delphic heights to climb,
Yet his were somehow nearer the sublime.
He spoke, and went again by the old way—
Not knowing it would be for the last time.

CAPUT MORTUUM

Nor even if with a wizard force I might
Have summoned whomsoever I would name,
Should anyone else have come than he who came,
Uncalled, to share with me my fire that night;
For though I should have said that all was right,
Or right enough, nothing had been the same
As when I found him there before the flame,
Always a welcome and a useful sight.

Unfailing and exuberant all the time,
Having no gold he paid with golden rhyme,
Of older coinage than his old defeat,
A debt that like himself was obsolete
In Art's long hazard, where no man may choose
Whether he play to win or toil to lose.

MONADNOCK THROUGH THE TREES

BEFORE there was in Egypt any sound
Of those who reared a more prodigious means
For the self-heavy sleep of kings and queens
Than hitherto had mocked the most renowned,—
Unvisioned here and waiting to be found,
Alone, amid remote and older scenes,
You loomed above ancestral evergreens
Before there were the first of us around.

And when the last of us, if we know how,
See farther from ourselves than we do now,
Assured with other sight than heretofore
That we have done our mortal best and worst,—
Your calm will be the same as when the first
Assyrians went howling south to war.

THE LONG RACE

UP THE old hill to the old house again
Where fifty years ago the friend was young
Who should be waiting somewhere there among
Old things that least remembered most remain,
He toiled on with a pleasure that was pain
To think how soon asunder would be flung
The curtain half a century had hung
Between the two ambitions they had slain.

They dredged an hour for words, and then were
done.
"Good-bye! . . . You have the same old weather-
vane—
Your little horse that's always on the run."
And all the way down back to the next train,
Down the old hill to the old road again,
It seemed as if the little horse had won.

MANY ARE CALLED

THE Lord Apollo, who has never died,
Still holds alone his immemorial reign,
Supreme in an impregnable domain
That with his magic he has fortified;
And though melodious multitudes have tried
In ecstasy, in anguish, and in vain,
With invocation sacred and profane
To lure him, even the loudest are outside.

Only at unconjectured intervals,
By will of him on whom no man may gaze,
By word of him whose law no man has read,
A questing light may rift the sullen walls,
To cling where mostly its infrequent rays
Fall golden on the patience of the dead.

HAUNTED HOUSE

Here was a place where none would ever come
For shelter, save as we did from the rain.
We saw no ghost, yet once outside again
Each wondered why the other should be dumb;
For we had fronted nothing worse than gloom
And ruin, and to our vision it was plain
Where thrift, outshivering fear, had let remain
Some chairs that were like skeletons of home.

There were no trackless footsteps on the floor
Above us, and there were no sounds elsewhere.
But there was more than sound; and there was more
Than just an axe that once was in the air
Between us and the chimney, long before
Our time. So townsmen said who found her there.

THE SHEAVES

WHERE long the shadows of the wind had rolled,
Green wheat was yielding to the change assigned;
And as by some vast magic undivined
The world was turning slowly into gold.
Like nothing that was ever bought or sold
It waited there, the body and the mind;
And with a mighty meaning of a kind
That tells the more the more it is not told.

So in a land where all days are not fair,
Fair days went on till on another day
A thousand golden sheaves were lying there,
Shining and still, but not for long to stay—
As if a thousand girls with golden hair
Might rise from where they slept and go away.

KARMA

CHRISTMAS was in the air and all was well
With him, but for a few confusing flaws
In divers of God's images. Because
A friend of his would neither buy nor sell,
Was he to answer for the axe that fell?
He pondered; and the reason for it was,
Partly, a slowly freezing Santa Claus
Upon the corner, with his beard and bell.

Acknowledging an improvident surprise,
He magnified a fancy that he wished
The friend whom he had wrecked were here again.
Not sure of that, he found a compromise;
And from the fulness of his heart he fished
A dime for Jesus who had died for men.

MAYA

THROUGH an ascending emptiness of night,
Leaving the flesh and the complacent mind
Together in their sufficiency behind,
The soul of man went up to a far height;
And where those others would have had no sight
Or sense of else than terror for the blind,
Soul met the Will, and was again consigned
To the supreme illusion which is right.

"And what goes on up there," the Mind inquired,
"That I know not already to be true?"—
"More than enough, but not enough for you,"
Said the descending Soul: "Here in the dark,
Where you are least revealed when most admired,
You may still be the bellows and the spark."

AS IT LOOKED THEN

In a sick shade of spruce, moss-webbed, rock-fed,
Where, long unfollowed by sagacious man,
A scrub that once had been a pathway ran
Blindly from nowhere and to nowhere led,
One might as well have been among the dead
As half way there alive; so I began
Like a malingering pioneer to plan
A vain return—with one last look ahead.

And it was then that like a spoken word
Where there was none to speak, insensibly
A flash of blue that might have been a bird
Grew soon to the calm wonder of the sea—
Calm as a quiet sky that looked to be
Arching a world where nothing had occurred.

SILVER STREET

Here, if you will, your fancy may destroy
This house before you and see flaming down
To ashes and to mysteries the old town
Where Shakespeare was a lodger for Mountjoy;
Here played the mighty child who for his toy
Must have the world—king, wizard, sage and clown,
Queen, fiend and trollop—and with no more
 renown,
May be, than friends and envy might annoy.

And in this little grave-yard, if you will,
He stands again, as often long ago
He stood considering what it signified.
We may have doubted, or be doubting still—
But whether it be all so, or all not so,
One has to walk up Wood Street from Cheapside.

A MAN IN OUR TOWN

We pitied him as one too much at ease
With Nemesis and impending indigence;
Also, as if by way of recompense,
We sought him always in extremities;
And while ways more like ours had more to please
Our common code than his improvidence,
There lurked alive in our experience
His homely genius for emergencies.

He was not one for men to marvel at,
And yet there was another neighborhood
When he was gone, and many a thrifty tear.
There was an increase in a man like that;
And though he be forgotten, it was good
For more than one of you that he was here.

EN PASSANT

I SHOULD have glanced and passed him, naturally,
But his designs and mine were opposite;
He spoke, and having temporized a bit,
He said that he was going to the sea:
"I've watched on highways for so long," said he,
"That I'll go down there to be sure of it."
And all at once his famished eyes were lit
With a wrong light—or so it was to me.

That evening there was talk along the shore
Of one who shot a stranger, saying first:
"You should have come when called. This afternoon
A gentleman unknown to me before,
With deference always due to souls accurst,
Came out of his own grave—and not too soon."

NOT ALWAYS

I

In surety and obscurity twice mailed,
And first achieving with initial rout
A riddance of weak fear and weaker doubt,
He strove alone. But when too long assailed
By nothing, even a stronger might have quailed
As he did, and so might have gazed about
Where he could see the last light going out,
Almost as if the fire of God had failed.

And so it was till out of silence crept
Invisible avengers of a name
Unknown, like jungle-hidden jaguars.
But there were others coming who had kept
Their watch and word; and out of silence came
A song somewhat as of the morning stars.

NOT ALWAYS

II

THERE were long days when there was nothing
said,
And there were longer nights where there was
nought
But silence and recriminating thought
Between them like a field unharvested.
Antipathy was now their daily bread,
And pride the bitter drink they daily fought
To throw away. Release was all they sought
Of hope, colder than moonlight on the dead.

Wishing the other might at once be sure
And strong enough to shake the prison down,
Neither believed, although they strove together,
How long the stolid fabric would endure
That was a wall for them, and was to frown
And shine for them through many sorts of
weather.

WHY HE WAS THERE

Much as he left it when he went from us
Here was the room again where he had been
So long that something of him should be seen,
Or felt—and so it was. Incredulous,
I turned about, loath to be greeted thus,
And there he was in his old chair, serene
As ever, and as laconic and as lean
As when he lived, and as cadaverous.

Calm as he was of old when we were young,
He sat there gazing at the pallid flame
Before him. "And how far will this go on?"
I thought. He felt the failure of my tongue,
And smiled: "I was not here until you came;
And I shall not be here when you are gone."

GLASS HOUSES

LEARN if you must, but do not come to me
For truth of what your pleasant neighbor says
Behind you of your looks or of your ways,
Or of your worth and virtue generally;
If he's a pleasure to you, let him be—
Being the same to him; and let your days
Be tranquil, having each the other's praise,
And each his own opinion peaceably.

Two others once did love each other well,
Yet not so well but that a pungent word
From each came stinging home to the wrong ears.
The rest would be an overflow to tell,
Surely; and you may slowly have inferred
That you may not be here a thousand years.

THE LAGGARDS

Scorners of earth, you that have one foot shod
With skyward wings, but are not flying yet,
You that observe no goal or station set
Between your groping and the towers of God
For which you languish, may it not be odd
And avaricious of you to forget
Your toll of an accumulating debt
For dusty leagues that you are still to plod?

But many have paid, you say, and paid again;
And having had worse than death are still alive,
Only to pay seven fold, and seven times seven.
They are many; and for cause not always plain,
They are the laggards among those who strive
On earth to raise the golden dust of heaven.

NEW ENGLAND

HERE where the wind is always north-north-east
And children learn to walk on frozen toes,
Wonder begets an envy of all those
Who boil elsewhere with such a lyric yeast
Of love that you will hear them at a feast
Where demons would appeal for some repose,
Still clamoring where the chalice overflows
And crying wildest who have drunk the least.

Passion is here a soilure of the wits,
We're told, and Love a cross for them to bear;
Joy shivers in the corner where she knits
And Conscience always has the rocking-chair,
Cheerful as when she tortured into fits
The first cat that was ever killed by Care.

"IF THE LORD WOULD MAKE WINDOWS IN HEAVEN"

She who had eyes but had not wherewithal
To see that he was doomed to his own way,
Dishonored his illusions day by day,
And year by year was more angelical.
Flaunting an injured instinct for the small,
She stifled always more than she would say;
Nursing a fear too futile to betray,
She sewed, and waited for the roof to fall.

A seer at home, she saw that his high lights
That were not shining, and were not afire,
Were such as never would be seen from there;
A saint abroad, she saw him on the heights,
And feared for him—who, if he went much higher,
Might one day not be seen from anywhere.

BATTLE AFTER WAR

Out of a darkness, into a slow light
That was at first no light that had a name,
Like one thrust up from Erebus he came,
Groping alone, blind with remembered sight.
But there were not those faces in the night,
And all those eyes no longer were aflame
That once he feared and hated, being the same
As his that were the fuel of his fright.

He shone, for one so long among the lost,
Like a stout Roman after Pentecost:
"Terror will yield as much as we dare face
Ourselves in it, and it will yield no more,"
He said. And we see two now in his place,
Where there was room for only one before.

THE GARDEN OF THE NATIONS

(1923)

WHEN we that are the bitten flower and fruit
Of time's achievement are undone between
The blight above, where blight has always been,
And the old worm of evil at the root,
We shall not have to crumble destitute
Of recompense, or measure our chagrin;
We shall be dead, and so shall not be seen
Amid the salvage of our disrepute.

And when we are all gone, shall mightier seeds
And scions of a warmer spring put forth
A bloom and fruitage of a larger worth
Than ours? God save the garden, if by chance,
Or by approved short sight, more numerous weeds
And weevils be the next inheritance!

REUNION

By some derision of wild circumstance
Not then our pleasure somehow to perceive,
Last night we fell together to achieve
A light eclipse of years. But the pale chance
Of youth resumed was lost. Time gave a glance
At each of us, and there was no reprieve;
And when there was at last a way to leave,
Farewell was a foreseen extravagance.

Tonight the west has yet a failing red,
While silence whispers of all things not here;
And round there where the fire was that is dead,
Dusk-hidden tenants that are chairs appear.
The same old stars will soon be overhead,
But not so friendly and not quite so near.

A CHRISTMAS SONNET

For One in Doubt

While you that in your sorrow disavow
Service and hope, see love and brotherhood
Far off as ever, it will do no good
For you to wear his thorns upon your brow
For doubt of him. And should you question how
To serve him best, he might say, if he could,
"Whether or not the cross was made of wood
Whereon you nailed me, is no matter now."

Though other saviors have in older lore
A legend, and for older gods have died—
Though death may wear the crown it always wore,
And ignorance be still the sword of pride—
Something is here that was not here before,
And strangely has not yet been crucified.